Poptropica® English Islands

TEST BOOKLET

1

Pearson

Contents

Introduction

Evaluation can be described as an attempt to analyse the learning that a pupil has achieved over a period of time as a result of the classroom teaching/learning situation. It plays an integral part in the teaching and learning process.

The evaluation material in this Test Booklet has been designed to analyse pupils' progress, with the aim of reinforcing the positive aspects and identifying areas for improvement.

There are five main reasons for evaluation:

Formative – to increase motivation by making evaluation a part of the continuous learning process.

Summative – to give pupils feedback on their progress or achievement at a particular point in time, often formally through tests.

Informative – to give pupils and parents feedback on progress or achievements.

Diagnostic – to monitor individual pupils' needs and help identify pupils who need special support.

Evaluative – to identify pupils' level of achievement and select or order pupils according to merit, to check effectiveness of teaching methods, teaching materials and teachers.

This Test Booklet contains one Placement test, eight Unit tests, three End of term tests, one Final test, and one Exam preparation test.

The Placement test can be used as a diagnostic test at the start of the year, reviewing learning from the previous year and helping to assess pupils' ability.

The Unit tests can be used at the end of each unit, to monitor pupils' progress through the course, to give pupils feedback on their achievement and to identify areas requiring reinforcement.

The End of term and Final tests can be used as informative and evaluative tests, for reporting purposes.

The Exam preparation test can be used to help prepare pupils for external exams such as CYLETS and Trinity.

A and B versions have been provided for the Unit tests, the Final test and the Exam preparation test. Both versions cover exactly the same learning objectives, and will provide an equal level of evaluation. You may find it useful to hand out different A and B versions to students who sit next to each other. Alternatively, you could use the A version to test the whole class and use the B version for reinforcement purposes.

The four skills of Reading, Writing, Listening and Speaking are tested through self-explanatory activities that students will be familiar with from their work in class.

Each activity has its own score, with a consolidated score at the end of each page and a total score at the end of each test. Points have been allocated according to the number of tasks pupils are required to do in each activity.

For Speaking activities, points have been allocated according to the learning objectives. In the lower levels of the course, points should be awarded for correct word identification. In the higher levels of the course, longer answers are expected, and points should be awarded for production of the target language. Pupils should be allowed to make more than one attempt, and you should encourage them to self-correct.

Procedure on the day before the evaluation

- Review unit content using games to give practice for the coming evaluation.
- Ask pupils to predict what they think the content of the evaluation might be, using L1 as needed.

Procedure on the day of evaluation

- Play a game, and sing a song or chant to help pupils to move from L1 to English.
- Play the audio and direct pupils to complete the listening activities. Audio files are available on the Active Teach, or at pearsonelt.com/islands.
- As with the audio throughout this course, you may wish to pause the audio to allow pupils to complete each question.
- Depending on your classroom setup, you may wish to set pupils up in pairs to complete the speaking activity and monitor the class as a whole. Alternatively, you may prefer to have pupils speak individually to you while the remainder of the class works through the reading and writing exercises.
- Have some small pieces of scrap paper available for students to make notes for their speaking evaluation. Emphasise that they only should make notes. Try to avoid full sentences or scripts being written.
- Set pupils a time limit within which to complete the remainder of the test.
- Pupils will need colouring pens or pencils for some of the activities.
- Check the answers against the Answer Key on pages 72–75. Please note that the answers for the speaking activities are intended as suggested answers only. Write the total score in the space provided at the bottom of each page and at the end of the tests.
- When handing tests back to pupils, go through the answers and explain any errors.

Poptropica English Islands also encourages the practice of self-evaluation, which is provided at the end of each unit in the Activity Book. This gives the pupils an important opportunity to express their own opinion about their progress in English.

Placement

1 Read and match. (4 points)

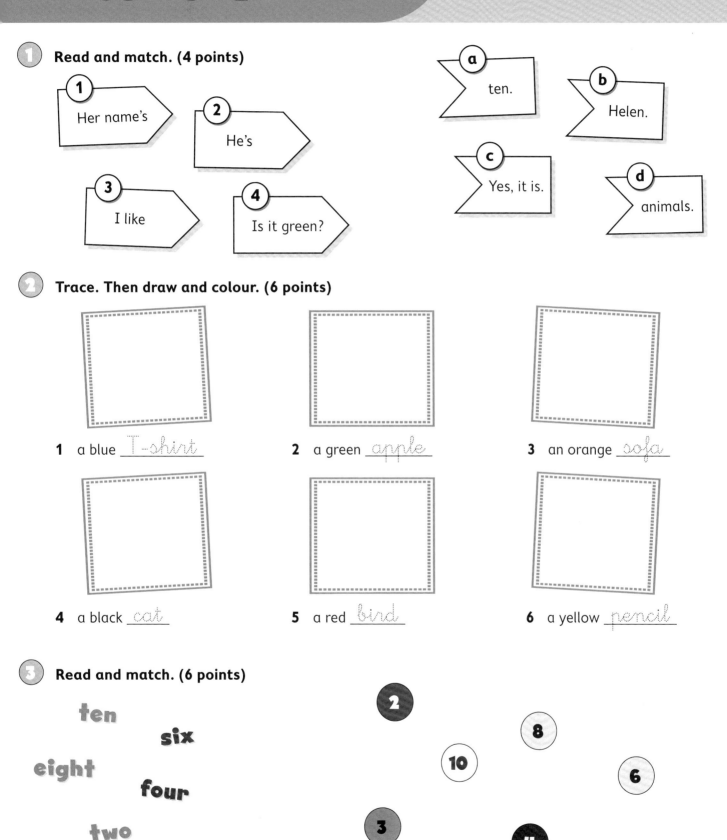

1 Her name's

2 He's

3 I like

4 Is it green?

a ten.

b Helen.

c Yes, it is.

d animals.

2 Trace. Then draw and colour. (6 points)

1 a blue ‾T-shirt‾

2 a green ‾apple‾

3 an orange ‾sofa‾

4 a black ‾cat‾

5 a red ‾bird‾

6 a yellow ‾pencil‾

3 Read and match. (6 points)

ten   six   eight   four   two   three

2   8   10   6   3   4

Score: ___ /16

Placement

1 **Listen and match. (4 points)**

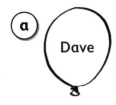 Dave
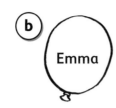 Emma
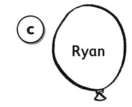 Ryan
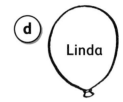 Linda

 **1**

 **2**

 **3**

 **4**

2 **Listen. Then draw and colour. (4 points)**

 **1**

 **2**

 **3**

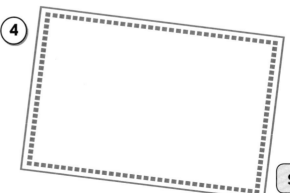 **4**

Score: ___ /8

1 Look and talk. What's in the pictures? (6 points)

Score: ___ /6

Whole test score: ___ /30

1 **Write. Then match and trace. (6 points)**

name   old   What's

1   How _____ are you?

2   What's your _____?

3   _____ your favourite colour?

a   _My favourite colour is blue_ .

b   _My name's George_ .

c   _I'm six_ .

2 **Read and colour. (5 points)**

1   My flower is purple and orange.

2   Look at my leaf. It's grey.

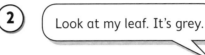
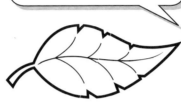

3   The fish is pink and black.

4   The bird is black and white.

5   Look at my butterfly. It's pink and brown.

3 **Look and match. (4 points)**

1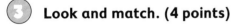

2

3

4

climb

walk

hop

dance

Score: ____ /15

My birthday

1 Listen and colour. (4 points)

1

2

3

4

  2 Listen and circle. (5 points)

1 Jim is (six / seven).

2 Simon's favourite colour is (blue / brown).

3 Anne is (six / seven).

4 Flora's favourite colour is (orange / purple).

5 Tom's favourite colour is (green / grey).

3 Ask and answer about you. (6 points)

What's your name?

How old are you?

What's your favourite colour?

Score: ___ /15

Whole test score: ___ /30

1 Write. Then match and trace. (6 points)

| What's   colour   How |

1 _____ your name?   a   <u>It's red</u> .

2 _____ old are you?   b   <u>My name's Clara</u> .

3 What _____ is it?   c   <u>I'm seven</u> .

2 Read and colour. (5 points)

1 Look at my fish. It's pink.

2  Look at my bird. It's grey and white.

3  The flower is purple and orange.

 **4** The butterfly is orange and black.

5  The leaf is grey and brown.

3 Look and match. (4 points)

1

run

stamp

2

clap

3

jump

4

Score: ____ /15

1 **Listen and colour. (4 points)**

①

②

③

④

2 **Listen and circle. (5 points)**

1 Jim's favourite colour is (green / blue).

2 Simon is (seven / eight).

3 Anne's favourite colour is (purple / pink).

4 Flora is (ten / nine).

5 Tom is (eight / nine).

3 **Ask and answer about you. (6 points)**

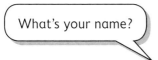

What's your name?

How old are you?

What's your favourite colour?

Score: ___ /15

Whole test score: ___ /30

1 Read and match. (4 points)

What's this, Ben?

What are these?

It's a ruler.
It's a yellow ruler.

It's a pencil sharpener.
It's white.

They're pens. A green pen,
a red pen and a black pen.

They're pencils. They're blue.

1 The pens are   **a**   pencils.

2 It's a white   **b**   green, red and black.

3 They're blue   **c**   yellow.

4 The ruler is   **d**   pencil sharpener.

2 Read and write. (6 points)

| this   many   It's   are   guitar   brown |

1 How _____ chairs can you see?

2 It's a red _____.

3 What _____ these?

4 What's _____?

5 The tables are _____.

6 _____ a drum.

3 Read and draw. (5 points)

This is a music lesson.

Draw six drums. They're red and white.

Draw a black and white piano.

Draw the teacher.

Score: ___ /15

Listen and number. (4 points)

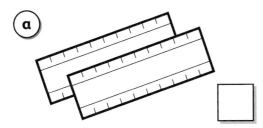 a

 b

c

d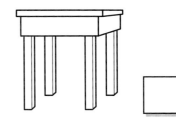

  Listen and circle. (5 points)

1 2 desks / a desk
2 chairs / a chair
3 15 rubbers / 5 rubbers
4 14 tables / 16 tables
5 9 pencils / 19 pencils

3 **Look and talk. What's in your classroom? (6 points)**

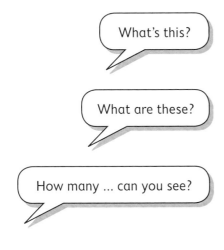

What's this?

What are these?

How many ... can you see?

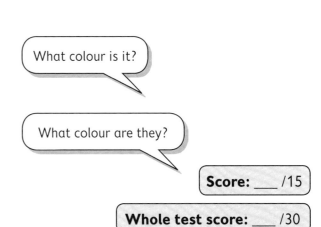

What colour is it?

What colour are they?

Score: ___ /15

Whole test score: ___ /30

1 **Read and match. (4 points)**

What's this, Ben?

What are these?

It's a pencil case.
It's a yellow pencil case.

This is a pen.
It's pink.

They're rubbers. A blue rubber,
a pink rubber and a green rubber.

They're pencil sharpeners.
They're orange.

1 It's a yellow	**a** pencil sharpeners.
2 The pen is	**b** blue, pink and green.
3 The rubbers are	**c** pink.
4 They're orange	**d** pencil case.

2 **Read and write. (6 points)**

piano   these   How   They're   brown   colour

1 _____ many books can you see?   **2** It's a _____.

3 What are _____?   **4** _____ violins.

5 What _____ are they?   **6** They're _____.

3 **Read and draw. (5 points)**

This is a music lesson.

Draw four guitars. They're pink
and green.

Draw a brown violin.

Draw the teacher.

Score: ____ /15

1 **Listen and number. (4 points)**

 a

b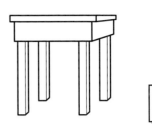

c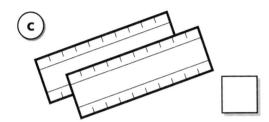

d

2 **Listen and circle. (5 points)**

1 a desk / 2 desks

2 a chair / chairs

3 5 rubbers / 4 rubbers

4 16 tables / 17 tables

5 19 pencils / 9 pencils

3 **Look and talk. What's in your classroom? (6 points)**

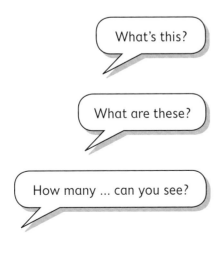

What's this?

What are these?

How many ... can you see?

What colour is it?

What colour are they?

Score: ___ /15

Whole test score: ___ /30

1 **Read and circle. (4 points)**

Hi! I'm Emma and I'm six.
This is my sister. Her name's Wendy.
This is my brother. His name's Ben.
Wendy is eight. Ben is nine.
This is my friend. His name's Bob.
He's seven.

1 Is Emma six?   Yes, she is. / No, she isn't.

2 Is Wendy nine?   Yes, she is. / No, she isn't.

3 Is Ben eight?   Yes, he is. / No, he isn't.

4 Is Bob seven?   Yes, he is. / No, he isn't.

2 **Read and number. (5 points)**

a This is my grandad. He's a cook. ☐

b My brother is a dentist. ☐

c My dad is a farmer. ☐

d This is my sister. She's a dancer. ☐

e My friend is a pilot. ☐

① **②** **③** **④** **⑤**

3 **Read and write. (6 points)**

| Yes   he   isn't   is   Is she   This |

1 **a** This _____ my mum.

b _____ an artist?

c No, she _____.
She's a dentist.

2 **a** _____ is my dad.

b Is _____ a pilot?

c _____, he is.

Score: ___ /15

1 **Listen and number. (5 points)**

 a

 b

 c

 d

 e

2 **Listen and circle *True* or *False*. (4 points)**

1	Pete is a dentist.	True / False
2	His mum is a cook.	True / False
3	Mary is 18.	True / False
4	His dad is a farmer.	True / False

3 **Look and say. (6 points)**

My family

sister

grandad

dad

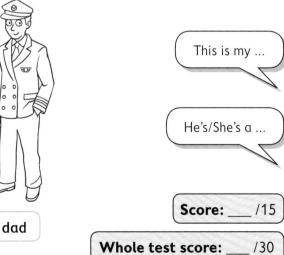

This is my …

He's/She's a …

Score: ___ /15

Whole test score: ___ /30

1 Read and circle. (4 points)

My name's Pete. I'm seven.
This is my brother. His name's Liam.
This is my sister. Her name's Jill.
Liam is ten. Jill is four.
This is my friend. Her name's Sue.
She's seven.

1 Is Pete six?	Yes, he is. / No, he isn't.
2 Is Liam ten?	Yes, he is. / No, he isn't.
3 Is Jill four?	Yes, she is. / No, she isn't.
4 Is Sue eight?	Yes, she is. / No, she isn't.

2 Read and number. (5 points)

a This is my sister. She's a dancer. ☐

b My friend is a pilot. ☐

c My brother is a dentist. ☐

d This is my grandad. He's a cook. ☐

e My dad is a farmer. ☐

3 Read and write. (6 points)

> isn't   Yes   is   he   This   Is she

1

a _____ is my grandad.

b Is _____ a doctor?

c No, he _____. He's a teacher.

2

a This _____ my granny.

b _____ a cook?

c _____, she is.

Score: ___ /15

 PHOTOCOPIABLE

1 Listen and number. (5 points)

 a

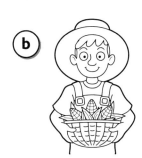 b

 c

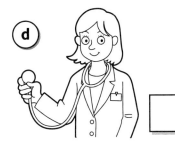 d

 e

 **2 Listen and circle *True* or *False*. (4 points)**

1	Pete is 19.	True / False
2	His mum is a vet.	True / False
3	Mary is a cook.	True / False
4	His dad is a teacher.	True / False

3 Look and say. (6 points)

 *My family*

 dad

 mum

 brother

This is my ...

He's/She's a ...

Score: ___ /15

Whole test score: ___ /30

1 **Read and write. (4 points)**

> I've   got   She's   has

1 This is my friend, Sue. _____ got five red legs.

2 Grandad has _____ seven toes!

3 Look! Granny _____ got pink feet.

4 I'm Patrick. _____ got four purple heads and six toes.

2 **Read and number. Then colour. (10 points)**

a I'm Angela. I've got a red T-shirt. ☐

b I'm Helen. I've got blue trousers. ☐

c This is Tom. He's got an orange and yellow jumper. ☐

d This is my dad. He's got black shoes. ☐

e Granny's got a purple and pink hat. ☐

1 **2** **3** **4** **5**

3 **Draw a friend and write. (6 points)**

This is my friend.

His/Her name's _____.

He's/She's got _____.

_____

_____

_____

_____

_____

Score: ____ /20

Poptropica English Islands – Test Booklet 1

 1 **Listen and circle** *True* **or** *False*. **(5 points)**

1	Gus has got six green feet.	True / False
2	Johnny's got a purple tail.	True / False
3	Sandy's got seven white feet.	True / False
4	Mandy's got twelve arms.	True / False
5	Thomas has got three red fingers.	True / False

2 **Listen and circle. (4 points)**

1 His (trousers / shoes) are blue.

2 She's got a (green / red) dress.

3 He's got a (yellow / grey) jumper.

4 Her (arms / hands) are dirty.

3 **Draw your body and clothes. Then say. (6 points)**

I've got ...

It's/They're ...

Score: ___ /15

Whole test score: ___ /35

1 **Read and write. (4 points)**

has I've He's got

1 I'm Nick. _____ got seven red arms.

2 This is my friend, Tom. _____ got six white feet and eight toes.

3 This is my sister. She's _____ one purple head and five orange legs.

4 Look! Mum _____ got six green toes.

2 **Read and number. Then colour. (10 points)**

a I'm Tina. I've got two red shoes. ☐

b I'm Rob. I've got green trousers. ☐

c This is Gavin. He's got blue and white socks. ☐

d My mum's got a yellow and orange skirt. ☐

e This is my sister. She's got a blue T-shirt. ☐

1 **2** **3** **4** **5**

3 **Draw yourself and write. (6 points)**

This is me.

My name's _____.

I've got _____.

_____

_____

_____

_____

_____

Score: ____ /20

4 My body

1 **Listen and circle *True* or *False*. (5 points)**

1	Gus has got seven red feet.	True / False
2	Johnny's got a purple head.	True / False
3	Sandy's got seven yellow feet.	True / False
4	Mandy's got green arms.	True / False
5	Thomas has got three red legs.	True / False

2 **Listen and circle. (4 points)**

1 He's got (purple / blue) trousers.

2 Her dress is (red / pink).

3 His (T-shirt / jumper) is yellow.

4 She's got dirty (hands / legs).

3 **Draw a monster and its clothes. Then say. (6 points)**

He's/She's got …

It's/They're …

Score: ___ /15

Whole test score: ___ /35

5 Pets

1 Look and write. (5 points)

| snake   tortoise   cat   rabbit   parrot |

1    **2**    **3**   **4**    **5**

_____   _____   _____   _____   _____

2 Read and circle. (4 points)

1 A hamster has got a (long / short) tail.

2 A chick has got (small / big) wings.

3 A puppy is (an old / a young) dog.

4 A frog has got (fat / thin) legs.

3 Draw a pet and write. (6 points)

It's a _____

_____.

It's _____

_____.

It's got _____

_____.

Score: ___ /15

     PHOTOCOPIABLE

1 **Listen and circle *True* or *False*. (4 points)**

1 It's got two big legs.   True / False
2 It's got two small arms.   True / False
3 It's got a small white tail. True / False
4 It's got a grey body.   True / False

2 **Listen and match. (5 points)**

3 **Look and say. (6 points)**

He's/She's got …

It's got …

It's a …

Score: ___ /15

Whole test score: ___ /30

1 **Look and write. (5 points)**

| mouse   rabbit   dog   tortoise   parrot |

1   2   3   4   5

_____ _____ _____ _____ _____

2 **Read and circle. (4 points)**

1 A mouse is a (big / small) pet.

2 A cat is (a young / an old) kitten.

3 A snake has got a (long / short) body.

4 A bird has got (thin / fat) legs.

3 **Draw a pet and write. (6 points)**

It's a _____

_____.

It's _____

_____.

It's got _____

_____.

Score: ___ /15

Poptropica English Islands – Test Booklet 1

PHOTOCOPIABLE

5 Pets

 1 **Listen and circle *True* or *False*. (4 points)**

1	It's got two big feet.	True / False
2	It's got two big arms.	True / False
3	It's got a small brown tail.	True / False
4	It's got a white body.	True / False

 2 **Listen and match. (5 points)**

 3 **Look and say. (6 points)**

He's/She's got …

It's got …

It's a …

Score: ___ /15

Whole test score: ___ /30

1 **Read and write. (4 points)**

sofa window bed door

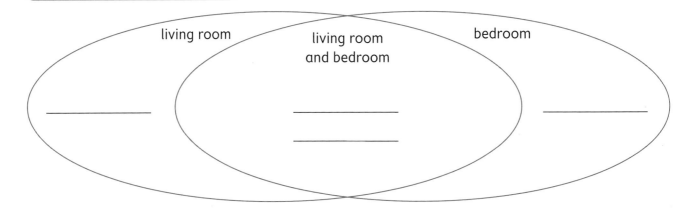

living room   living room and bedroom   bedroom

_____   _____   _____

_____

2 **Read and circle. (5 points)**

1 **a** (Where's / Where are) the parrot? **b** (They're / It's) in the bathroom.

2 **a** (Where's / Where are) Laura and Sam? **b** (They're / She's) in the living room. They're (in / on) the sofa.

3 **Draw your kitchen and write. (6 points)**

In my kitchen, there's a _____

_____.

There's a _____

_____.

There are _____

_____.

Score: ___ /15

1 Listen and ✓ or ✗. (5 points)

Granny   Tom

Janet

Ben

Mum   Dad

1 ☐   2 ☐   3 ☐   4 ☐   5 ☐

2 Listen and circle. (4 points)

1 ⓐ    ⓑ    2 ⓐ    ⓑ

3 ⓐ 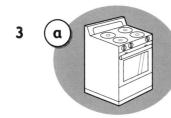   ⓑ 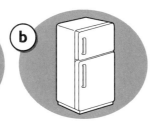   4 ⓐ 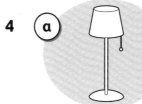   ⓑ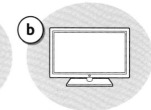

3 Look at the picture in Activity 1 and talk. (6 points)

Where's/Where are ...?   There's/There are ...   It's in/on/under ...

Score: ___ /15

Whole test score: ___ /30

1 Read and write. (4 points)

cooker   bath   sink   door

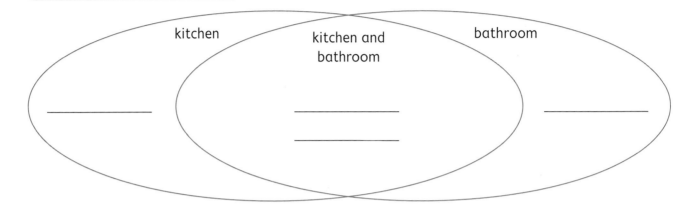

kitchen   kitchen and
bathroom   bathroom

_____   _____

_____

2 Read and circle. (5 points)

1 **a** (Where's / Where are) Diane?   **b** (She's / It's) in the living room.

2 **a** (Where's / Where are) the cats?   **b** (It's / They're) in the bedroom.
                                                     They're (in / under) the bed.

3 Draw your living room and write. (6 points)

In my living room, there's a _____

_____.

There's a _____

_____.

There are _____

_____.

Score: ___ /15

1 Listen and ✓ or ✗. (5 points)

Mum   Dad

Granny   Tom

Ben

Janet

 1 ☐   2 ☐   3 ☐   4 ☐   5 ☐

2 Listen and circle. (4 points)

1 (a) 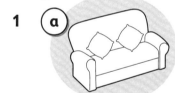   (b)    2 (a)    (b)

3 (a) 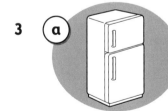   (b) 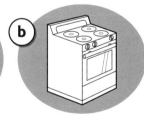   4 (a)    (b)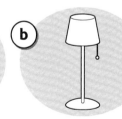

3 Look at the picture in Activity 1 and talk. (6 points)

Where's/Where are ...?   There's/There are ...   It's in/on/under ...

Score: ____ /15

Whole test score: ____ /30

1 **Look and match. (5 points)**

①  ② 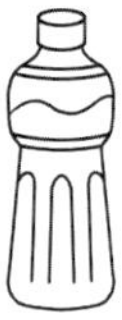 ③  ④  ⑤

| juice | cheese | bread | water | cake |

2 **Look. Then circle and write. (6 points)**

1 MILK  ☺ I (like / don't like) _____.

2 ☹ I (like / don't like) _____.

3 ☺ I (like / don't like) _____.

3 **Draw and write. (4 points)**

I like _____.

_____

_____

I don't like _____.

_____

_____

Score: ___ /15

  PHOTOCOPIABLE

 **7 Food**

 1 Listen and ✓ or ✗. (6 points)

1  ⓐ   ⓑ  MILK

2 ⓐ    ⓑ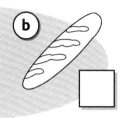

3 ⓐ 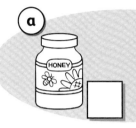 HONEY   ⓑ

2 Listen and match. (4 points)

honey

chocolate ice cream

 Ben

 Jill

sandwich

chocolate cake

3 Draw food that's good/bad for you and say. (5 points)

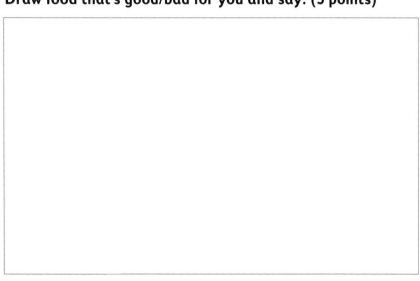

 ... is good for me.

... is bad for me.

Score: ___ /15

Whole test score: ___ /30

1 **Look and match. (5 points)**

(1)  (2)  (3)  (4)  (5)

| chocolate | milk | fish | jelly | honey |

2 **Look. Then circle and write. (6 points)**

1   I (like / don't like) _____.

2   I (like / don't like) _____.

3   I (like / don't like) _____.

3 **Draw and write. (4 points)**

_____ is good for me.

_____ is bad for me.

Score: _____ /15

Listening and speaking B

1 Listen and ✓ or ✗. (6 points)

1 a  b  2 a b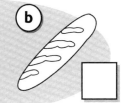

3 a  b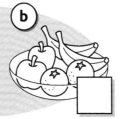

 2 Listen and match. (4 points)

Jill   Ben

3 Draw food that you like/don't like and say. (5 points)

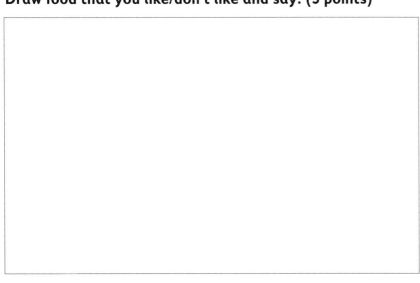 

I don't like ...

Score: ___ /15

Whole test score: ___ /30

1 **Read and match. (6 points)**

1 Where's my bed?	**a** I'm hungry.
2 Argh! A big, angry dog!	**b** I'm thirsty.
3 Water, please!	**c** I'm scared.
4 It's my birthday. I've got ten presents.	**d** I'm sad.
5 Mmm ... Bread and cheese!	**e** I'm happy.
6 I'm ill. My friends are in the garden. I'm in bed!	**f** I'm tired.

2 **Read and write. (5 points)**

> I am   Is   they aren't   he isn't   Are

1 Are you hungry? Yes, _____.

2 _____ Rob angry? No, _____. He's bored.

3 _____ you happy? Yes, I am.

4 Are Sam and Tim bored? No, _____. They're sad.

3 **Draw and write. (4 points)**

> hot   cold   tired   angry

I'm _____

_____

_____.

I'm not _____

_____

_____.

Score: ___ /15

1 **Listen and circle. (4 points)**

1 **a**  **b**    **2** **a**  **b**

3 **a**  **b**    **4** **a**  **b**

2 **Listen and circle *True* or *False*. (5 points)**

1 He's thirsty.   True / False
2 She's hungry.   True / False
3 He's hurt.   True / False
4 She's scared.   True / False
5 He's hungry.   True / False

3 **Look at the picture and talk. (6 points)**

Is he/she ...?   Are they ...?   I'm ...

Score: ____ /15

Whole test score: ____ /30

1 **Read and match. (6 points)**

1 Where's my jumper and hat?   **a** I'm hurt.
2 Open the window, please.   **b** I'm cold.
3 Ouch! My finger!   **c** I'm bored.
4 That's my cake! Stop!   **d** I'm ill.
5 My body hurts. I'm in bed.   **e** I'm hot.
6 Have you got a game?   **f** I'm angry.

2 **Read and write. (5 points)**

I'm not   he isn't   Is   they aren't   they are

1 Are Sam and Tim scared? No, _____.
2 Are Anna and Jo excited? Yes, _____.
3 _____ Mike tired? No, _____. He's bored.
4 Are you bored? No, _____.

3 **Draw and write. (4 points)**

thirsty   hungry   scared   hurt

I'm _____

_____

_____.

I'm not _____

_____

_____.

Score: ___ /15

1 Listen and circle. **(4 points)**

1 (a)  (b)

2 (a)  (b)

3 (a)  (b)

4 (a)  (b)

2 Listen and circle *True* or *False*. **(5 points)**

1 He's tired.   True / False

2 She's happy.   True / False

3 He's bored.   True / False

4 She's angry.   True / False

5 He's hungry.   True / False

3 Look at the picture and talk. **(6 points)**

Is he/she ...?   Are they ...?   I'm ...

Score: ____ /15

Whole test score: ____ /30

1 Read and match. (4 points)

1	How old are you?	a	Purple.
2	What's your name?	b	My name's Jenny.
3	What's this?	c	I'm ten.
4	What's your favourite colour?	d	It's a pencil sharpener.

2 Read and draw. (6 points)

1 What's this?
It's a yellow leaf.

2 What are these?
They're chairs.

3 How many rulers can you see?
Eight.

4 Is your sister a doctor?
Yes, she is.

5 What colour is the butterfly?
It's orange and purple.

6 Is your grandad a cook?
Yes, he is.

Score: ___ /10

End of term 1

Units 1–3
Reading and writing

3 **Read. Then look and circle *True* or *False*. (4 points)**

1

2

3

4

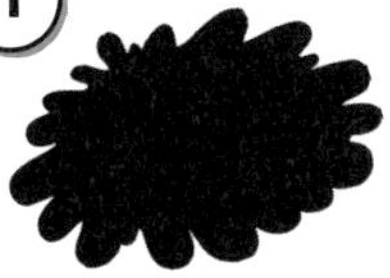

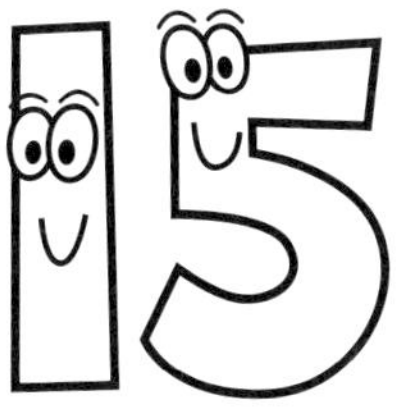

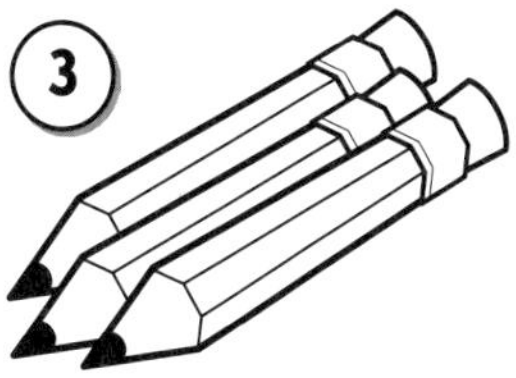

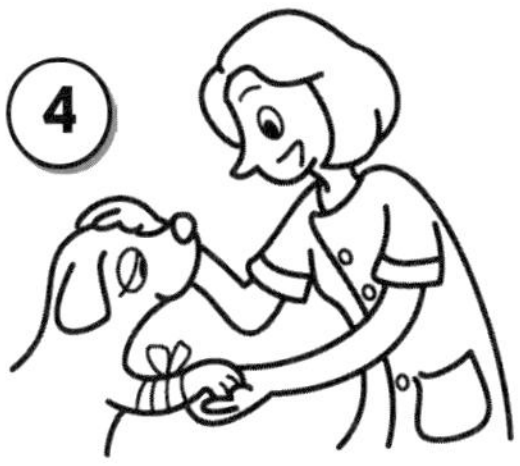

1 My favourite colour is black. True / False
2 My sister is sixteen. True / False
3 They're pens. True / False
4 She's a vet. True / False

4 **Read and write. (5 points)**

drum
violin
brother
mum
piano

Music	**Family**
______________	______________
______________	______________
______________	

5 **Draw two people from your family. Then write. (6 points)**

Her name's ______________________________.

She's __________________________________.

His name's ______________________________.

He's ___________________________________.

Score: ___ /15

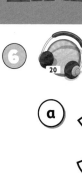 **6** **Listen and colour. (4 points)**

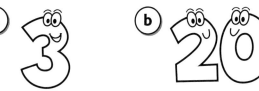 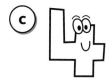 

 7 **Listen and write. (6 points)**

> violin   pink   seven   guitar   eight   black

EMMA

She's ¹ _____.

Favourite colour: ² _____

Favourite instrument: ³ _____

JOHN

He's ⁴ _____.

Favourite colour: ⁵ _____

Favourite instrument: ⁶ _____

8 **Draw your desk and classroom objects. Then say. (5 points)**

What are these?

What's this?

What colour are they?

What colour is it?

Score: ___ /15

© **Pearson Education Limited** 2017   PHOTOCOPIABLE

9 **Listen and match. (5 points)**

1    **2** 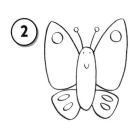   **3**    **4**    **5**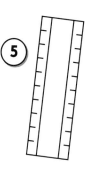

a    **b**   **c**   **d**   **e**

10 **Listen and circle. (4 points)**

1 Harry is his (dad / grandad).
   He's (an artist / a teacher).

2 Mary is his (mum / sister).
   She's a (teacher / dancer).

11 **Look and say. (6 points)**

  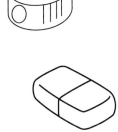  

He's/She's a …

It's a …/They're …

Score: ___ /15

Whole test score: ___ /55

End of term 2

1 **Read and match. (4 points)**

1 Have you got a pet spider?

2 What's that?

3 What are those?

4 Where's your cat?

a It's a frog.

b Yes, I have.

c She's on my bed!

d They're parrots.

2 **Read and draw. (6 points)**

1 What's that?
It's a small mouse.
It's got a long tail.

2 What are those?
They're lamps.
There are three lamps.

3 Where are my socks?
They're under the bed.

4 Have you got a pet hamster?
Yes, I have. It's a fat hamster.

5 Where's Anne?
She's on the sofa in the living room.

6 Look! My hands are dirty.

Score: ___ /10

3 **Read. Then look and circle *True* or *False*. (4 points)**

1   He's got a dirty face.   True / False
2   There's a window in the living room.   True / False
3   There's a kitten on my bed.   True / False
4   I've got three toes.   True / False

4 **Read and write. (5 points)**

sofa
TV
cooker
lamp
fridge

Living room

_____

_____

_____

Kitchen

_____

_____

5 **Draw your favourite pet. Circle and write. (6 points)**

This is my favourite pet.

His / Her name is _____.

His / Her colour is _____.

He's / She's _____.

Score: ___ /15

6 **Listen and match. (4 points)**

a

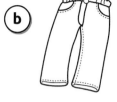
b

Sarah

Nick

c

d

7 **Listen and circle *True* or *False*. (6 points)**

1	His granny's got a blue hat.	True / False
	She's got twenty chicks.	True / False
2	She's got a pet hamster.	True / False
	Her pet is in the living room.	True / False
3	Aunt Lisa is in the kitchen.	True / False
	George and Sue are in the garden.	True / False

8 **Draw and colour. Then say. (5 points)**

tail wings T-shirt jumper
hat dress trousers

He's/She's got …

Score: ___ /15

9 **Listen and draw. (4 points)**

10 **Listen and circle. (6 points)**

1 There are four (frogs / dogs) in the garden.

2 She's got a pink (skirt / dress).

3 It's got three legs and fourteen (fingers / toes).

4 There's one (big / small) window in the bathroom.

5 Her friends are in the (café / library).

6 He's got (a young / an old) tortoise.

11 **Look at the picture in Activity 9. Ask and answer. Then say. (5 points)**

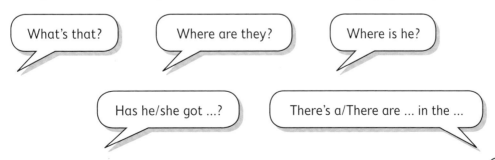

What's that?

Where are they?

Where is he?

Has he/she got ...?

There's a/There are ... in the ...

Score: ___ /15

Whole test score: ___ /55

1 **Read and match. (4 points)**

1	Do you like honey?	a	No, they aren't.
2	Is Ben cold?	b	Yes, I do.
3	Are you sad?	c	No, I'm not. I'm ill.
4	Are they angry?	d	Yes, he is.

2 **Read and draw. (6 points)**

1 What do you like for lunch?
I like chicken and salad.

2 Do you like bread?
Yes, I do.

3 Are you happy?
Yes, I am.

4 Is Dave hungry?
No, he isn't. He's thirsty.

5 Do you like fish?
No, I don't. I like ice cream.

6 Are you scared?
No, I'm not. I'm sad.

Score: ___ /10

End of term 3

3 **Read. Then look and circle _True_ or _False_. (4 points)**

1	**2**	**3**	**4**

1 I don't like salad. True / False
2 It's cold. True / False
3 He's hurt. True / False
4 She's scared. True / False

4 **Read and write. (5 points)**

water
chocolate
jelly
milk
juice

Drink

_____

_____

_____

Eat

_____

_____

5 **Draw your packed lunch. Circle and write. (6 points)**

This is my packed lunch.

It is _____ and _____.

It is good / bad for me.

I like _____.

I don't like _____.

Score: ___ /15

6 🎧 28 **Listen and number. (6 points)**

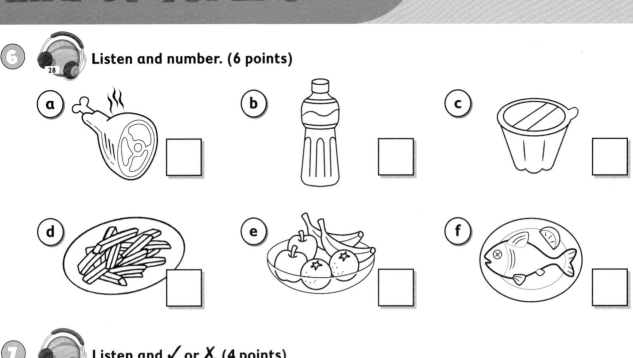

a   □

b   □

c   □

d   □

e   □

f   □

7 🎧 29 **Listen and ✓ or ✗. (4 points)**

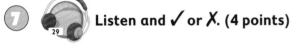

1 a □   b HONEY □

2 a □   b MILK □

8 **Look. Then ask and answer. (5 points)**

Do you like ...?

Is ... good/bad for you?

Score: ____ /15

9 **Listen and circle. (5 points)**

1 (a)   (b)   2 (a)   (b)   3 (a)  (b)

4 (a)   (b)   5 (a)   (b)

10 **Listen and write. (4 points)**

sad   happy   scared   tired

(1) Grandad's _____.

(2)  My dog's _____.

(3)  My rabbit's _____.

(4) She's _____.

11 **Look. Then ask and answer. (6 points)**

Is he/she ...?

Are they ...?

Score: ____ /15

Whole test score: ____ /55

1 **Read and draw. (5 points)**

This is my classroom.
There are eleven tables in the classroom.
There is a big window.

There's a guitar on the teacher's table.
I've got my school books on my table.
My ruler is in my pencil case.

2 **Read and circle *True* or *False*. (5 points)**

My house has got a big garden. There are pink and purple flowers.
There are red and blue butterflies.
I've got a pet cat. She's got a long, white tail. She's in the garden.
There are fifteen birds. Birds are her favourite food! She's hungry.
The birds are scared ... and I'm angry!

1 In the garden, there are flowers and butterflies.   True / False
2 The cat's got a brown tail.   True / False
3 The cat is in the garden.   True / False
4 There are five birds.   True / False
5 The cat's angry.   True / False

Score: ___ /10

1 **Read and write. (5 points)**

> There's   They're   has got   Where's   this

1 What's _____?

2 He _____ a red jumper.

3 _____ pencils.

4 _____ my cake?

5 _____ a lamp on the desk.

2 **Draw your favourite room and write. (10 points)**

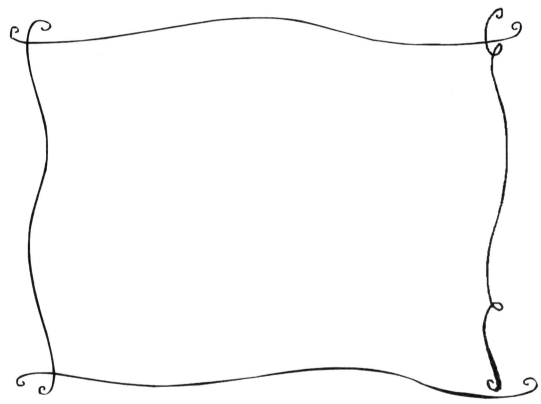

This is my favourite room.

This is my _____.

There's _____.

There are _____.

They're _____.

It's _____.

Score: ___ /15

  Listen and circle *True* or *False*. (6 points)

1	Harry is nine.	True / False
2	He's got one sister.	True / False
3	His mum is a cook.	True / False
4	Ben's got a pet hamster.	True / False
5	Harry's got a guitar.	True / False
6	Mark's got three small drums.	True / False

  Listen and draw. (4 points)

  Listen and match. (10 points)

park

shop

library

café

playground

Daisy

Jamie

Belinda

Steve

Phil

ruler

flowers

book

dogs

sandwich

Score: ____ /20

1 **Find five differences. (10 points)**

Picture A

Picture B

Is there a/an ...?

Where's the ...?

Is the ... in/on/ under the ...?

I can see ...

The ... is in/on/ under ...

There's/There are ...

The man is ...

Score: ___ /10

Whole test score: ___ /55

1 Read and draw. (5 points)

This is my bedroom.
There is a small window.
I've got a big bed and a table.

There's a lamp on the table.
There are two books under my bed.
My hat is on the chair.

2 Read and circle *True* or *False*. (5 points)

This is my garden. There are ten trees in the garden. They are tall.
There are red flowers and white flowers. There are eleven birds.
I've got a pet dog. He's black and white. He's tired. He's under a tree.
It's hot and I'm hungry. I've got sandwiches and my favourite juice.

1 There are small trees.		True / False
2 There are eleven birds in the garden.		True / False
3 The dog is hungry.		True / False
4 The dog's under a tree.		True / False
5 I've got chicken and vegetables.		True / False

Score: ___ /10

1 Read and write. (5 points)

> There's   this   Where's   has got   They're

1 _____ your brother?

2 She _____ a red hat.

3 _____ pencils.

4 What's _____ ?

5 _____ a cake in the kitchen.

2 Draw your favourite pet and write. (10 points)

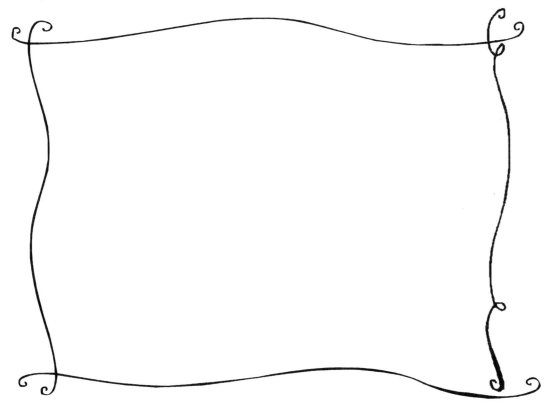

This is my favourite pet.

This is _____.

It's got _____.

It likes _____.

It's _____.

It's _____.

Score: ____ /15

  Listen and circle *True* or *False*. (6 points)

1 Harry's got two brothers.   True / False
2 His dad is a cook.   True / False
3 Harry's got a pet hamster.   True / False
4 His mum and dad have got two big cats.   True / False
5 The piano is in his bedroom.   True / False
6 Harry likes the drums.   True / False

  Listen and draw. (4 points)

  Listen and match. (10 points)

library   **Daisy**   sandwich

park   **Jamie**   book

shop   **Belinda**   flowers

playground   **Steve**   ruler

café   **Phil**   dogs

Score: ___ /20

1 **Find five differences. (10 points)**

Picture A

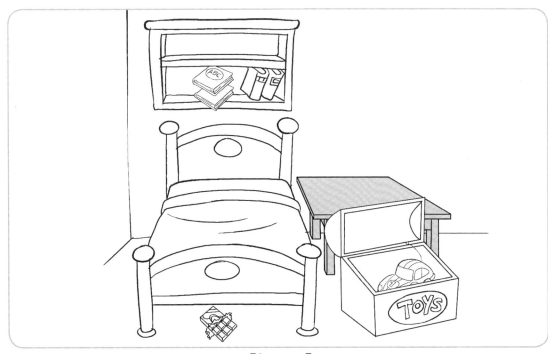

Picture B

Is there a/an ...?

Where's the ...?

Is the ... in/on/ under the ...?

I can see ...

The ... is in/on/ under ...

There's/There are ...

Score: ____ /10

Whole test score: ____ /55

1 Look and read. Then ✓ or ✗. (3 points)

1 This is a drum. ☐

2 This is a sink. ☐

3 This is a tortoise. ☐

2 Read and write. (5 points)

| meat four tail thirsty park |

I've got ¹ _____ legs and
a short ² _____. I like milk and
³ _____. I'm ⁴ _____.
Where's my water? I'm in the ⁵ _____.
I'm happy!

Score: ____ /8

© Pearson Education Limited 2017   PHOTOCOPIABLE

3 Look at the pictures. Then look at the letters and write the words. (5 points)

1 _____ i o d w w n

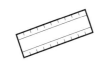

2 _____ r e l r u

3 _____ l a s d a

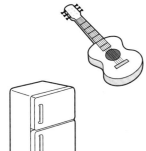

4 _____ g r i a t u

5 _____ g f d i e r

4 Look at the picture. Then read the questions and write one-word answers. (5 points)

1 What's under the table?

_____

2 Where is the bird?

_____ the table

3 How many chairs can you see?

_____

4 Can you see a door in the picture?

_____

5 Is there a window in the picture?

_____

Score: ____ /10

1 **Listen and draw lines. (4 points)**

2 **Read the questions. Then listen and answer. (5 points)**

1 What's Sandra's sister's name? _____

2 How old is she? _____

3 What's Sandra's brother's name? _____

4 How many people are there in Sandra's family? _____

5 How many hamsters has Sandra got? _____

Score: ___ /9

3 **Listen and ✓. (2 points)**

1 What can Bill do?

2 What has Mary got?

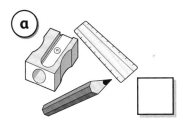 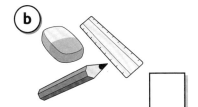 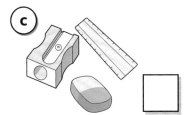

4 **Listen and colour. (5 points)**

Score: ____ /7

1 Look and read. Then ✓ or ✗. (3 points)

1 This is a chick. ☐

2 This is jelly. ☐

3 This is a bed. ☐

2 Read and write. (5 points)

legs   white   favourite   jump   vegetables

I am [1] _____. I've got four short
[2] _____. I like [3] _____.
My [4] _____ food is carrots.
I [5] _____ and hop and run.

Score: ___ /8

3 Look at the pictures. Then look at the letters and write the words. (5 points)

1 _____   e s o h u

2 _____   d b e r a

3 _____   r o d o

4 _____   g i h t e

5 _____   k m l i

4 Look at the picture. Then read the questions and write one-word answers. (5 points)

1 What pet is in the picture?

   a _____

2 Are Mum and Millie in the garden?

   _____

3 What's in the bathroom?

   a _____

4 Has Millie got dirty feet?

   _____

5 Has Mum got trousers?

   _____

Score: ____ /10

1 **Listen and draw lines. (4 points)**

2 **Read the questions. Then listen and answer. (5 points)**

1 What's Sandra's sister's name? _____

2 How old is she? _____

3 What's Sandra's brother's name? _____

4 How many people are there in Sandra's family? _____

5 How many cats has Sandra got? _____

Score: ____ /9

Exam preparation

3 Listen and ✓. (2 points)

1 What can Bill do?

2 What has Mary got?

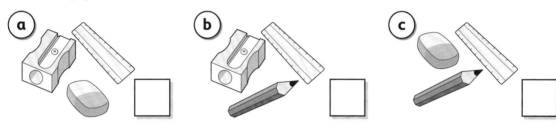

4 Listen and colour. (5 points)

Score: ___ /7

1 **Look and talk about the picture. (6 points)**

What is this/that?

Where is the ...?

I can see ...

There's/There are ...

He's/She's got ...

He's/She's/It's ...

Score: ___ /6

2 **Look and talk about the picture. (6 points)**

Where's the ...?

I can see ...

The ... is in/on/under ...

There's/There are ...

He's/She's got ...

He's/She's/It's ...

Score: ___ /6

3 **Look and talk about your classroom. (6 points)**

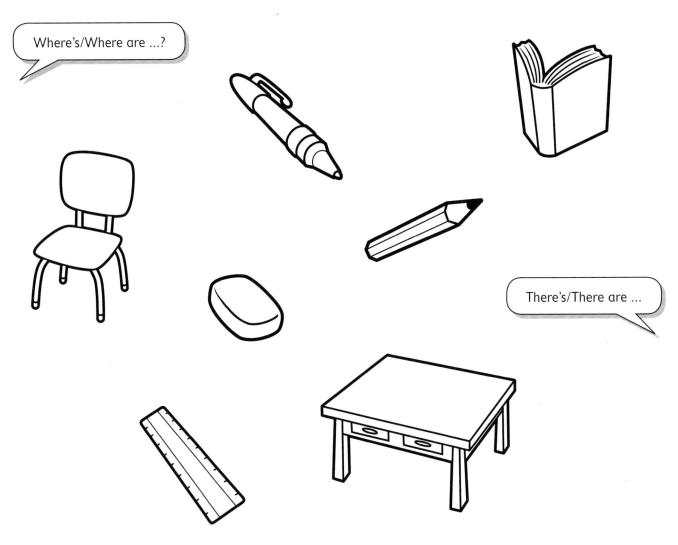

Where's/Where are ...?

There's/There are ...

4 **Ask and answer. (6 points)**

- name
- age
- clothes
- favourite food

Score: ___ /12

5 Look at the picture and tell your friend to do the different actions/feelings. **(6 points)**

6 Look again at Activity 5 and point. Then ask your friend. **(6 points)**

Score: ___ /12

Whole test score: ___ /70

Answer Key

Placement

Reading and writing

1 **1** b **2** a **3** d **4** c

2 (pictures)

3 ten – 10   six – 6   eight – 8   four – 4
two – 2   three – 3

Listening

1 **1** b **2** d **3** a **4** c

2 **1** a brown dog **2** a long, thin, pink fish
3 a small green leaf **4** a blue bird

Speaking

1 (example answers) **a** He's got a pet. It's a mouse.
He likes fruit. He's got an apple./**b** He's in the kitchen.
He's sad. He likes ice cream./**c** She's got a cat. She's got
long hair. She's happy.

Unit 1

Reading and writing A

1 **1** old, c **2** name, b **3** What's, a

2 (colouring) **1** purple and orange **2** grey **3** pink and
black **4** black and white **5** pink and brown

3 **1** hop **2** climb **3** dance **4** walk

Listening and speaking A

1 **1** purple and orange **2** green **3** black
4 brown and red

2 **1** seven **2** brown **3** six **4** orange **5** green

3 (example answers) My name's … I'm (six).
My favourite colour is (blue)./It's (blue).

Reading and writing B

1 **1** What's, b **2** How, c **3** colour, a

2 (colouring) **1** pink **2** grey and white **3** purple and
orange **4** orange and black **5** grey and brown

3 **1** stamp **2** jump **3** clap **4** run

Listening and speaking B

1 **1** purple and orange **2** green **3** black
4 brown and red

2 **1** blue **2** eight **3** purple **4** ten **5** nine

3 (example answers) My name's … I'm (six).
My favourite colour is (green)./It's (green).

Unit 2

Reading and writing A

1 **1** b **2** d **3** a **4** c

2 **1** many **2** guitar **3** are **4** this **5** brown **6** It's

3 (picture)

Listening and speaking A

1 **a** 1 **b** 3 **c** 4 **d** 2

2 **1** a desk **2** chairs **3** 5 rubbers **4** 16 tables
5 9 pencils

3 (example answers) It's a (pencil). It's (yellow).
They're (chairs). They're (green). Twelve.

Reading and writing B

1 **1** d **2** c **3** b **4** a

2 **1** How **2** piano **3** these **4** They're **5** colour
6 brown

3 (picture)

Listening and speaking B

1 **a** 3 **b** 2 **c** 1 **d** 4

2 **1** a desk **2** chairs **3** 5 rubbers **4** 16 tables
5 9 pencils

3 (example answers) It's a (pencil). It's (yellow).
They're (chairs). They're (green). Twelve.

Unit 3

Reading and writing A

1 **1** Yes, she is. **2** No, she isn't. **3** No, he isn't.
4 Yes, he is.

2 **a** 3 **b** 2 **c** 5 **d** 4 **e** 1

3 **1a** is **1b** Is she **1c** isn't **2a** This **2b** he **2c** Yes

Listening and speaking A

1 **a** 5 **b** 3 **c** 2 **d** 1 **e** 4

2 **1** False **2** False **3** True **4** True

3 (example answers) This is my (sister/grandad/dad).
He's/She's a(n) (dancer/artist/pilot).

Reading and writing B

1 **1** No, he isn't. **2** Yes, he is. **3** Yes, she is.
4 No, she isn't.

2 **a** 4 **b** 1 **c** 2 **d** 3 **e** 5

3 **1a** This **1b** he **1c** isn't **2a** is **2b** Is she **2c** Yes

Listening and speaking B

1 **a** 1 **b** 5 **c** 4 **d** 3 **e** 2

2 **1** False **2** True **3** True **4** False

3 (example answers) This is my (dad/mum/brother).
He's/She's a (cook/doctor/artist).

Unit 4

Reading and writing A
1 **1** She's **2** got **3** has **4** I've
2 **a** 3 **b** 4 **c** 1 **d** 2 **e** 5 (and colouring)
3 (open answers)

Listening and speaking A
1 **1** False **2** False **3** True **4** True **5** False
2 **1** trousers **2** red **3** yellow **4** hands
3 (example answers) I've got (clean hands). I've got (a T-shirt). It's (red). I've got (socks). They're (white).

Reading and writing B
1 **1** I've **2** He's **3** got **4** has
2 **a** 4 **b** 1 **c** 5 **d** 2 **e** 3 (and colouring)
3 (open answers)

Listening and speaking B
1 **1** False **2** True **3** False **4** True **5** True
2 **1** blue **2** red **3** jumper **4** hands
3 (example answers) He's/She's got (one eye). It's (orange). He's/She's got (six toes). They're (purple).

Unit 5

Reading and writing A
1 **1** cat **2** parrot **3** snake **4** tortoise **5** rabbit
2 **1** short **2** small **3** a young **4** thin
3 (open answers)

Listening and speaking A
1 **1** False **2** True **3** True **4** False
2 boy – a, b
   girl – c, d, e
3 (example answers) He's/She's got (a dog). It's got (short legs). It's a (small) dog.

Reading and writing B
1 **1** dog **2** rabbit **3** tortoise **4** parrot **5** mouse
2 **1** small **2** an old **3** long **4** thin
3 (open answers)

Listening and speaking B
1 **1** True **2** False **3** False **4** True
2 boy – c, e
   girl – a, b, d
3 (example answers) He's/She's got (a dog). It's got (long legs). It's a (thin) dog.

Unit 6

Reading and writing A
1 living room – sofa
   bedroom – bed
   living room and bedroom – window, door
2 **1a** Where's **1b** It's **2a** Where are **2b** They're, on
3 (open answers)

Listening and speaking A
1 **1** ✓ **2** ✗ **3** ✗ **4** ✗ **5** ✓
2 **1** a **2** b **3** a **4** a
3 (example questions and answers) Where is (Ben)? (He's) in the (bathroom). Where are (Mum and Dad)? They're in the (kitchen). There is (a teddy bear). It's (on the bed). There are (two paintings). They're (on the wall).

Reading and writing B
1 kitchen – cooker
   bathroom – bath
   kitchen and bathroom – sink, door
2 **1a** Where's **1b** She's
   2a Where are **2a** They're, under
3 (open answers)

Listening and speaking B
1 **1** ✓ **2** ✗ **3** ✗ **4** ✗ **5** ✓
2 **1** b **2** a **3** b **4** b
3 (example questions and answers) Where is (Ben)? (He's) in the (bathroom). Where are (Mum and Dad)? They're in the (kitchen). There is (a teddy bear). It's (on the bed). There are (two paintings). They're (on the wall).

Unit 7

Reading and writing A
1 **1** bread **2** cake **3** water **4** juice **5** cheese
2 **1** like, milk **2** don't like, fish **3** like, honey
3 (open answers)

Listening and speaking A
1 **1** a ✗, b ✓ **2** a ✗, b ✓ **3** a ✗, b ✓
2 Jill – sandwich, honey
   Ben – chocolate ice cream, chocolate cake
3 (example answers) (Salad/Juice) is good for me. (Chocolate/Cake) is bad for me.

Reading and writing B
1 **1** milk **2** jelly **3** honey **4** chocolate **5** fish
2 **1** like, cheese **2** don't like, fruit **3** don't like, bread
3 (open answers)

Listening and speaking B
1 **1** a ✓, b ✗ **2** a ✗, b ✓ **3** a ✓, b ✗
2 Jill – sandwich, honey
   Ben – chocolate ice cream, chocolate cake
3 (example answers) I like (ice cream/cheese/honey). I don't like (milk/yoghurt/sausages).

Unit 8

Reading and writing A

1 1 f 2 c 3 b 4 e 5 a 6 d

2 1 I am 2 Is, he isn't 3 Are 4 they aren't

3 (open answers)

Listening and speaking A

1 1 b 2 a 3 b 4 b

2 1 True 2 False 3 False 4 True 5 True

3 (example questions and answers) Is he/she (happy)? (Yes, he/she is./No, he/she isn't.) Are they (hungry)? (Yes, they are./No, they aren't.) I'm (tired).

Reading and writing B

1 1 b 2 e 3 a 4 f 5 d 6 c

2 1 they aren't 2 they are 3 Is; he isn't 4 I'm not

3 (open answers)

Listening and speaking B

1 1 a 2 b 3 a 4 a

2 1 False 2 False 3 True 4 False 5 True

3 (example questions and answers) Is he/she (happy)? (Yes, he/she is./No, he/she isn't.) Are they (hungry)? (Yes, they are./No, they aren't.) I'm (tired).

End of term 1

Reading and writing

1 1 c 2 b 3 d 4 a

2 (pictures)

3 1 True 2 False 3 False 4 True

4 Music – drum, violin, piano
Family – brother, mum

5 (open answers)

Listening and speaking

6 1 red 2 purple 3 orange 4 yellow

7 1 eight 2 pink 3 guitar 4 seven 5 black 6 violin

8 (example answers) It's a (pencil case). It's (red and pink). They're (pens). They're (black).

9 1 c 2 a 3 b 4 e 5 d

10 1 grandad, an artist 2 sister, dancer

11 (example answers) He's/She's a (doctor/vet). It's a (pencil sharpener/rubber). Dance./Jump.

End of term 2

Reading and writing

1 1 b 2 a 3 d 4 c

2 (pictures)

3 1 True 2 False 3 False 4 True

4 Living room – TV, sofa, lamp
Kitchen – cooker, fridge

5 (open answers)

Listening and speaking

6 Sarah – b, d
Nick – a, c

7 1 False, True 2 False, True 3 True, False

8 (example answers) He's/She's got (three wings). They're (big). He's/She's got (a hat). It's (orange).

9 Pictures should show a T-shirt on the bed, two socks under the sink, a TV under the lamp and a kitten on a chair in the kitchen.

10 1 frogs 2 skirt 3 toes 4 big 5 library 6 an old

11 (example answers) It's a (lamp). They're (pictures). He's in the kitchen. They're in the living room. Yes, he/she has./No, he/she hasn't. There's (a mirror in the bathroom). There are (four chairs in the kitchen).

End of term 3

Reading and writing

1 1 b 2 d 3 c 4 a

2 (pictures)

3 1 True 2 False 3 True 4 False

4 Drink – water, milk, juice
Eat – chocolate, jelly

5 (open answers)

Listening and speaking

6 a 2 b 6 c 5 d 1 e 4 f 3

7 1 a ✓, b ✗ 2 a ✗, b ✗

8 (example questions and answers) Do you like (meat)? Yes, I do./No, I don't. Is (water good) for you? Is (chocolate bad) for you? Yes, it is./No, it isn't.

9 1 a 2 a 3 b 4 b 5 b

10 1 happy 2 tired 3 scared 4 sad

11 (example questions and answers) Is he/she (scared)? Yes, he/she is./No, he/she isn't.

Final

Reading A

1 (picture)

2 1 True 2 False 3 True 4 False 5 False

Writing A

1 1 this 2 has got 3 They're 4 Where's 5 There's

2 (open answers)

Listening A

1 1 False 2 True 3 False 4 True 5 True 6 False

2 Picture should show a small rabbit on the sofa, a small chair under the lamp, white socks under the chair and a guitar on the chair.

3 Daisy – café, sandwich   Jamie – playground, ruler
Belinda – library, book   Steve – park, dogs
Phil – shop, flowers

Speaking A

1 (example questions and answers) Is there a cat in picture A? Yes, there is./Where is the mouse in picture B? Under the chair./I can see a girl./Is the cat under the table? Yes, it is in picture B./The girl is on the chair./There are three chairs./The man is happy in picture A.

Differences: **1** A = The cat is on the chair. B = The cat is under the table. **2** A = The mouse is under the table. B = The mouse is under the chair. **3** A = The girl's got a cake. B = The girl's got eggs. **4** A = There isn't a sandwich in the picture. B = There's a sandwich. **5** A = The man is happy. B = The man is angry.

Reading B

1 (picture)

2 **1** False **2** True **3** False **4** True **5** False

Writing B

1 **1** Where's **2** has got **3** They're **4** this **5** There's

2 (open answers)

Listening B

1 **1** True **2** True **3** False **4** False **5** False **6** True

2 Picture should show a small rabbit on the sofa, a small chair under the lamp, white socks under the chair and a guitar on the chair.

3 Daisy – café, sandwich   Jamie – playground, ruler
Belinda – library, book   Steve – park, dogs
Phil – shop, flowers

Speaking B

1 (example questions and answers) Is there a mouse in picture A? Yes, there is./Where's the chocolate? It's under the bed in picture B./Is the T-shirt under the bed in picture A? No, it isn't. It's on the bed./The car is in the box./There's a mouse on the table in picture A.

Differences: **1** A = There's a T-shirt on the bed. B = There isn't a T-shirt on the bed. **2** A = There isn't chocolate under the bed. B = There's chocolate under the bed. **3** A = There's a mouse on the table. B = There isn't a mouse on the table. **4** A = There are two cars. B = There's one car. **5** A = The table is white. B = The table is grey.

Exam preparation
Reading and writing A

1 **1** ✗ **2** ✗ **3** ✓

2 **1** four **2** tail **3** meat **4** thirsty **5** park

3 **1** window **2** ruler **3** salad **4** guitar **5** fridge

4 **1** dogs **2** on **3** two **4** no **5** yes

Listening A

1 bread – on the table under the window
honey – under the cupboard
juice – on the cupboard
meat – on the cooker

2 **1** Anna **2** seven **3** Alex **4** five **5** one

3 **1** b **2** a

4 **1** a red pencil under the flower
2 a blue pencil on the big table
3 a yellow pencil under the small table
4 a green pencil on the small table
5 a black pencil on the chair

Reading and writing B

1 **1** ✓ **2** ✗ **3** ✓

2 **1** white **2** legs **3** vegetables **4** favourite **5** jump

3 **1** house **2** bread **3** door **4** eight **5** milk

4 **1** cat **2** no **3** sink **4** yes **5** yes

Listening B

1 bread – on the table under the window
honey – under the cupboard
juice – on the cupboard
meat – on the cooker

2 **1** Anna **2** seven **3** Alex **4** five **5** two

3 **1** c **2** b

4 **1** a red pencil under the flower
2 a blue pencil on the big table
3 a yellow pencil under the small table
4 a green pencil on the small table
5 a black pencil on the chair

Speaking A and B

1 (example questions and answers) Where is the son? Here. (pointing) I can see a mum and a dad. There are three children. There's one baby. She's got short hair. He's got a T-shirt.

2 (example questions and answers) Where's the mouse? It's under the table. I can see a big hat. There are cakes on the table. She's got a dress. He's got short hair.

3 (example answers) In my classroom, there are ten books. There are twelve tables. They're brown. My ruler is on my table. It's green.

4 (example questions and answers) What's your name? My name's …/How old are you? I'm …/Have you got a dress? Yes, I have./No, I haven't./Do you like cheese? Yes, I do./No, I don't./What's your favourite food? I like ice cream.

5 (example answers) You're bored/thirsty/happy/scared. Jump./Clap./Stomp.

6 (example questions and answers) Is he bored? Yes, he is./No, he isn't. Is she happy? Yes, she is./No, she isn't.

Audioscript

Audio files are available on the Active Teach, or at pearsonelt.com/islands.

M: Man

W: Woman

Placement
Placement Test. Test Booklet.
Activity 1. Listen and match.

1

M: Hi, Emma. How do you spell your name?

W: E-M-M-A

M: That's E-M-M-A?

W: Yes. That's right!

M: Thanks.

2

M: Hi, Linda. How do you spell your name?

W: L-I-N-D-A

M: That's L-I-N-D-A?

W: Yes. That's right.

M: Thanks.

3

W: Hi, Dave. How do you spell your name?

M: D-A-V-E.

W: That's D-A-V-E?

M: Yes. That's right.

W: Thanks.

4

W: Hello, Ryan. How do you spell your name?

M: R-Y-A-N.

W: That's R-I-A-N?

M: No! R-Y-A-N.

W: Oh, R-Y-A-N.

Placement Test. Test Booklet.
Activity 2. Listen. Then draw and colour.

1

W: This is a picture of my pet dog. He's brown and his name's Joey. What's your picture Fred?

2

M: This is a picture of a fish. It's a pink fish. It's long and thin. Jenny, what's your picture?

3

W: My picture is of a leaf. It's a small green leaf. What about your picture, Sam?

4

M: My picture is of a bird. I like birds. This bird is a blue bird.

Unit 1
Unit 1 Tests A and B. Test Booklet.
Activity 1. Listen and colour.

1

M: Look at my backpack, Sally. It's purple and orange. My favourite colour is purple.

2

M: What colour is your backpack, Barbara?

W: My backpack is green. My favourite colour is green.

3

W: What colour is your backpack Freddie?

M: Black. My favourite colour is black. My backpack is black.

4

M: Look at my backpack! It's brown and red. My favourite colour is red.

Unit 1 Tests A and B. Test Booklet.
Activity 2. Listen and circle.

1

M1: How old are you, Jim?

M2: I'm seven years old.

M1: What's your favourite colour?

M2: My favourite colour is blue.

2

M2: How old are you, Simon?

M1: I'm eight years old.

M2: And what's your favourite colour?

M1: My favourite colour?

M2: Yes. What is it? Is it blue?

M1: No. No. My favourite colour is brown.

3

M: What about you? How old are you, Anne?

W: I'm six years old.

M: And what's your favourite colour?

W: I like pink. No ... I like purple! Purple is my favourite colour. Yes, it's purple.

4

W1: Flora, how old are you?

W2: I'm ten.

W1: Do you like purple?

W2: No, I don't. My favourite colour is orange.

W1: Orange?

W2: Yes, orange!

5

W: How old are you, Tom?

M: I'm nine years old.

W:	And what's your favourite colour?
M:	Green.
W:	Your favourite colour is grey?
M:	No, it isn't grey. It's green.

Unit 2
Unit 2 Tests A and B. Test Booklet.
Activity 1. Listen and number.

1
W1:	Hey Di. What are these?
W2:	These are rulers, Tessa.

2
W1:	And ... What's this?
W2:	It's a desk, Tessa! It's my desk!

3
W1:	And ... What's this?
W2:	This is my pencil. My school pencil!

4
W1:	Now ... Sit down on your chair!
W2:	Sit down on my chair?
W1:	Yes!

Unit 2 Tests A and B. Test Booklet.
Activity 2. Listen and circle.

1
M:	What's this?
W:	It's a desk.

2
M:	What are these?
W:	They're chairs.

3
M:	What are these?
W:	They're rubbers. They're five rubbers.

4
M:	What are these?
W:	They're tables, sixteen tables.

5
M:	What are these?
W:	They're pencils, nine pencils.

Unit 3
Unit 3 Tests A and B. Test Booklet.
Activity 1. Listen and number.

1
W:	Is your brother a cook?
M:	Yes, he is.

2
M:	This is my dad.

W:	Is he an artist?
M:	No, he isn't. He's a vet.

3
W:	Is your sister a dancer?
M:	No, she isn't. She's a doctor.

4
M:	This is my granny.
W:	Is she an artist?
M:	Yes, she is!

5
W:	Is your grandad a vet?
M:	No, he isn't. He's a farmer.

Unit 3 Tests A and B. Test Booklet.
Activity 2. Listen and circle *True* or *False*.

1
M:	This is my big brother, Pete. He's twenty. He's an artist.

2
M:	This is a photo of my mum. She's a vet. Look!

3
M:	This is my sister, Mary. She's eighteen. She's a cook.

4
M:	This is a photo of my dad. He's a farmer.

Unit 4
Unit 4 Tests A and B. Test Booklet.
Activity 1. Listen and circle *True* or *False*.

1
M:	Hi. I'm Gus. I've got six red feet.

2
M:	Hi. I'm Johnny. I've got a pink body and a purple head.

3
W:	Hi. I'm Sandy. I've got seven white feet.

4
W:	Hi. I'm Mandy. I've got twelve green arms.

5
M:	Hi. I'm Thomas. I've got three red legs.

Unit 4 Tests A and B. Test Booklet.
Activity 2. Listen and circle.

1
M:	I've got blue trousers.

2
W:	I've got a red dress.

3
M:	I've got a yellow jumper.

4
W:	I've got dirty hands!

Unit 5

Unit 5 Tests A and B. Test Booklet.
Activity 1. Listen and circle *True* or *False*.

1

M:　It's got two big feet.
　　　It's got two big feet.

2

M:　It's got two small arms.
　　　It's got two small arms.

3

M:　It's got a small white tail.
　　　It's got a small white tail.

4

M:　It's got a white body.
　　　It's got a white body.

Unit 5 Tests A and B. Test Booklet.
Activity 2. Listen and match.

1

W:　He's got two dogs.

2

W:　She's got two cats.

3

W:　She's got one tortoise.

4

W:　He's got two rabbits.

5

W:　She's got one parrot.

Unit 6

Unit 6 Tests A and B. Test Booklet.
Activity 1. Listen and ✓ or X.

1

M:　Janet is in the bedroom. She's on the bed.

2

M:　Janet has got a book. The book is under her bed.

3

M:　Ben is in the kitchen.

4

M:　There's a bath under the window.

5

M:　Granny is in the living room.

Unit 6 Tests A and B. Test Booklet.
Activity 2. Listen and circle.

1

W:　This is the bedroom. There's a chair and a bed.

2

W:　This is the bathroom. There's a sink. There isn't a bath.

3

W:　In the kitchen there's a sink and a cooker.

4

W:　In the living room, there's a lamp and a sofa. There isn't a TV.

Unit 7

Unit 7 Tests A and B. Test Booklet.
Activity 1. Listen and ✓ or X.

1

M:　I like juice. I don't like vegetables. My favourite food is cake ... and I like milk.

2

W:　I don't like chicken and sandwiches. I like bread. I don't like yoghurt.

3

M:　My favourite foods are salad and ice cream. I don't like fruit and I don't like honey.

Unit 7 Tests A and B. Test Booklet.
Activity 2. Listen and match.

M:　What food do you like, Jill?

W:　Umm ... I like sandwiches.

M:　I like chocolate ice cream.

W:　What's your favourite food?

M:　Ah. My favourite food is chocolate cake. What's your favourite food?

W:　Honey. My favourite food is honey.

Unit 8

Unit 8 Tests A and B. Test Booklet.
Activity 1. Listen and circle.

1

W:　Hi. I'm Mandy. Today, I'm really, really, happy. It's my birthday!

2

M:　Hi. I'm Oliver. I'm in my house; in the kitchen. Arghhh! There's a small, white mouse. Arghhh! I'm scared!

3

W:　Hi. I'm Helen. I'm angry. My brother's got my chocolate! I want my chocolate.

4

W:　Hi. I'm Sarah. It's hot. I'm thirsty. I want cold water.

Unit 8 Tests A and B. Test Booklet.
Activity 2. Listen and circle *True* or *False*.

1

W:　Do you want a chicken sandwich?

M:　No. I'm not hungry. I want orange juice.

2

M: Sue. Where are you?

W: I'm in my bed. I'm hot and tired and thirsty. I don't want food.

3

W: Hi Ben. Are you happy?

M: No!

W: Are you sad?

M: No.

W: Are you ill?

M: No.

W: Are you bored?

M: Yes.

4

W: Look! A big spider! Arghhhh!!!

5

M: I want a cheese sandwich and salad and an ice cream and cake.

W: Are you hungry?

M: Yes!!!

End of term 1
End of term Test 1. Units 1–3. Test Booklet. Activity 6. Listen and colour.

M: What colour is number three?

W: Number three is red.

M: OK.
Now, what about number twenty?

W: Number twenty?

M: Yes.

W: Number twenty is purple.

M: Thank you.
And, what colour is number four?

W: Number four is orange.

M: OK.
What about number seventeen? What colour is it?

W: Number seventeen is yellow.

M: OK. ... So number three is red, twenty is purple, four is orange, seventeen is yellow. Is that right?

W: Yes. That's right!

End of term Test 1. Units 1–3. Test Booklet. Activity 7. Listen and write.

1

M: Hello. What's your name?

W: My name's Emma.

M: How old are you, Emma?

W: I'm eight.

M: OK. What's your favourite colour?

W: It's pink.

M: And, what's your favourite instrument?

W: My favourite instrument is the guitar!

2

W: Hi. What's your name?

M: My name's John.

W: How old are you?

M: I'm seven.

W: OK. What's your favourite colour John?

M: My favourite colour is black!

W: OK! And, what's your favourite instrument?

M: The violin!

End of term Test 1. Units 1–3. Test Booklet. Activity 9. Listen and match.

1

M: How many pencils can you see?

W: Six.

2

M: And how many butterflies?

W: I can see sixteen butterflies!

3

M: What are these?

W: They're leaves. Eleven leaves.

4

M: And what are these?

W: They're pencil cases.

M: How many can you see?

W: Fourteen.

5

M: OK. How many rulers can you see?

W: Eighteen.

End of term Test 1. Units 1–3. Test Booklet. Activity 10. Listen and circle.

1

M: This is my grandad. His name's Harry.

W: Is he a teacher?

M: No, he isn't. He's an artist.

2

W: Who's this? Is she your mum?

M: No! She's my sister. Her name's Mary.

W: Oh. OK.

M: She's a dancer.

W: A teacher?

M: No, a dancer.

End of term 2

End of term Test 2. Units 4–6. Test Booklet.
Activity 6. Listen and match.

1

M: My sister's name is Sarah. She's five. She's got green trousers. They're clean. She's got a pet, too. It's a cat. It's white.

2

M: And this is my friend, Nick. He's eight and his favourite colour is purple. He's got a pet rabbit. It's white and brown. He's got purple shoes!

End of term Test 2. Units 4–6. Test Booklet.
Activity 7. Listen and circle *True* or *False*.

1

W: Have you got a hat, Ben?

M: No, I haven't. My granny's got a hat.

W: What colour is it?

M: It's red!

W: Is she an artist?

M: No, she isn't. She's a farmer. She's got a goose, twenty chicks and thirteen rabbits.

W: Wow!

2

M: Hello. What's your favourite pet?

W: The snake!

M: Really? Have you got a snake?

W: Yes, I have!

M: Where is it?

W: It's in the living room. Look!

M: Oh yes!

3

W: This is my bedroom. It's my favourite room. And this is the kitchen. My Aunt Lisa is in the kitchen. She's a cook! And that's the garden. I've got a brother and a sister. His name's George and her name's Sue. They're at the playground.

End of term Test 2. Units 4–6. Test Booklet.
Activity 9. Listen and draw.

1

M: In the bedroom there's a bed. There's a T-shirt on the bed.

2

M: This is the bathroom. In the bathroom there's a bath and a sink. There are two socks under the sink.

3

M: Granny's in the living room. She's on a chair. There's a sofa and a lamp in the living room. The TV is under the lamp. Grandad's on the sofa.

4

M: This is the kitchen. There's a cooker, a table and four chairs. There's a kitten on one chair.

End of term Test 2. Units 4–6. Test Booklet.
Activity 10. Listen and circle.

1

M: I live in a house. This is the garden. There are three dogs and four frogs in the garden!

2

W: This is my favourite dress. It's white and green. I've got a skirt, too. It's pink.

3

W: Look at my drawing. It's got three legs and fourteen toes. It's got four eyes and thirteen fingers!

4

W: This is the kitchen. There are three small windows. In the bathroom, there's one big window.

5

W: Tom and Lucy are my friends. They're in the library. I'm in the café.

6

M: This is my pet. It's a tortoise and his name's Simon. He's old!

End of term 3

End of term Test 3. Units 7–8. Test Booklet.
Activity 6. Listen and number.

1

W: Mmmm … I like chips!

2

M: Ew … I don't like meat …

3

W: I don't like fish.

4

M: I like fruit! Yummy!

5

W: I like jelly.

6

M: I like water!

End of term Test 3. Units 7–8. Test Booklet.
Activity 7. Listen and ✓ or X.

1

W: Hi. My name's Jenny. I like ice cream and milk. I don't like bread and honey.

2

M: My name's Tom. I don't like cake and milk. I like bread and ice cream.

End of term Test 3. Units 7–8. Test Booklet.
Activity 9. Listen and circle.

1

M: Are they happy?

W: Yes, they are.

2

W: This is my sister Helen. She's angry.

M: Is she sad?

W: No, she isn't.

3

M: I'm hot.

W: Are you thirsty?

M: No, I'm not.

4

W: Is your brother bored?

M: No, he isn't. He's hungry.

5

M: Are you ill?

W: Yes, I am.

M: Are you cold?

W: No, I'm hot ...

End of term Test 3. Units 7–8. Test Booklet.
Activity 10. Listen and write.

1

M: This is is my grandad. He's happy! He's got a new pet. It's a hamster.

2

W: I've got a pet dog. His name's Fluffy.

M: Is he thirsty?

W: No, he isn't. He's tired.

3

W: Is this your rabbit?

M: Yes, it is.

W: Is it cold?

M: No, it isn't. It's scared because there's a big cat!

4

M: This is Samantha. She's my friend.

W: Is she angry?

M: No, she isn't. She's sad.

Final

Final Tests A and B. Test Booklet.
Activity 1. Listen and circle *True* **or** *False*.

Hi. I'm Harry. I'm ten. I've got two brothers, Ben and Mark, and one sister, Harriet. My mum is a dancer and my dad is a cook. I've got a pet rabbit. His name is Bilbo. Ben's got a hamster. Her name is Jane. My mum and dad have got two big dogs. In the living room there's a piano. My guitar is under the piano. I want a drum. Mark's got three big drums! He likes music. My family likes music.

Final Tests A and B. Test Booklet.
Activity 2. Listen and draw.

This is my Grandad's farmhouse. I'm in the living room.

There is a small rabbit sitting on the sofa.

There is a small chair under the lamp.

Under the chair there are white socks.

On the chair there is a guitar.

Final Tests A and B. Test Booklet.
Activity 3. Listen and match.

1

W: Hi Sam. Where's Daisy?

M: Daisy?

W: Yes. Where is she?

M: She's in the café.

W: Is she hungry?

M: Yes, she is. She's got a sandwich.

2

W: Where's Jamie?

M: Jamie's at school.

W: Is he in class?

M: No. He's in the playground. He's got a ruler. Look!

W: Oh, yes, he's got a long shadow.

3

W: And, where's Belinda?

M: Belinda?

W: Yes. Where is she?

M: She's in the library.

W: Has she got a new library book?

M: Yes, she has.

4

W: Where's Steve? Is he at school?

M: No, he isn't. He's in the park.

W: Has he got a dog?

M: Yes, he has. He's got two dogs: a big dog and a small dog.

5

W: Is Phil in the living room?

M: No, he isn't.

W: Is he in the park?

M: No, he isn't.

W: Is he in the shop?

M: Yes, It's his mum's birthday.

W: Ah! He's in the flower shop. He's got flowers for his mum's birthday.

Exam preparation
Exam preparation Tests A and B. Test Booklet.
Activity 1. Listen and draw lines.

M1: Hi, Harry.

M2: Hi, Jo.

M1: I'm hungry. I want bread and honey.

M2: There's bread in the kitchen. It's on the table under the window.

M1: Where's the honey?

M2: It's under the cupboard.

M1: Oh yes. Are you hungry?

M2: No, I'm not. I'm thirsty. I want a drink.

M1: There's orange juice on the cupboard.

M2: Ah yes. Thanks. And do you want some meat?

M1: Yes ... bread, meat and honey. A meat and honey sandwich! Yum! Yum! Where's the meat?

M2: Ugh! I don't like meat and honey sandwiches. I like cheese salad sandwiches. The meat is on the cooker. Look! There's Mum ...

Exam preparation Tests A and B. Test Booklet.
Activity 2. Read the questions. Then listen and answer.

W1: Hi Sandra. What's your sister's name?

W2: Hi Sophie. My sister's name is Anna.

W1: How do you spell Anna?

W2: A-N-N-A.

W1: I like that name!

W1: How old is Anna?

W2: She's seven.

W1: Seven?

W2: Yes.

W1: What's your brother's name?

W2: His name is Alex.

W1: That's A-L-E-X?

W2: Yes.

W1: How many people are there in your family?

W2: Well ... there's Mum and Dad and Alex and Anna and me! So, that's five.

W1: Five?

W2: Yes, that's right. Oh ... and the pets!

W1: What pets have you got, Sandra?

W2: My family has got two dogs, two cats, a hamster and a rabbit.

W1: Wow! That's a lot of pets!

W1: Have you got a favourite pet?

W2: That's a hard question. I like them all. Jimmy, the brown dog, is a happy dog. He's my favourite.

Exam preparation Tests A and B. Test Booklet.
Activity 3. Listen and ✓.

1 What can Bill do?

W: Hi Bill.

M: Hi Daisy.

W: Listen to the music. Look at me stamp my foot. One, two, three, four. Come on, Bill. Stamp your foot with me!

M&W: One, two, three, four.

2 What has Mary got?

W1: Have you got a pencil, Mary?

W2: Yes, I have. Here you are.

W1: Have you got a ruler, Mary?

W2: Yes, I have. Here you are.

W1: Have you got a pencil case, Mary?

W2: No, I haven't.

W1: Have you got a rubber, Mary?

W2: No, I haven't.

W1: Have you got a pencil sharpener, Mary?

W2: Yes, I have. Here you are.

W1: Thank you, Mary.

Exam preparation Tests A and B. Test Booklet.
Activity 4. Listen and colour.

W: Look. This is my classroom. What a mess!

M: Pens, pencils and rulers everywhere!

1

W: Where are the pencils? Can you see the pencils?

M: I can see a red pencil.

W: Where is the red pencil?

M: It's under the flower.

W: Ah yes. There's a book and a flower and a pencil.

M: Yes. That's right. The pencil is red.

2

W: Where is the blue pencil?

M: The blue pencil? Mmm. Ah, There it is.

W: Where?

M: There. On the big table.

W: There's a pen, a book, two rubbers and a blue pencil! Oh yes. I can see it now.

3

W: Is there a green pencil?

M: No, there isn't.

W: What's that under the small table?

M: It's a pencil.

W: Is it a green pencil?

M: No, it isn't. It's a yellow pencil.

4

W: Where's the green pencil, then?

M: It isn't under the small table and it isn't under the big table.

W: Look! There it is!

M: Where?

W: There, on the small table.

M: Oh yes. There's a pen, a ruler and a green pencil.

5

W: Where's my favourite pencil?

M: What colour is your favourite pencil?

W: My favourite pencil is black!

M: Black?

W: Yes, black!

M: There's a black pencil on the chair.

W: Where?

M: The chair under the big table. There is a black pencil on that chair.

W: Ah, yes. That's it. That's my favourite pencil. Thank you.

Evaluation chart

PUPIL'S NAME	EVALUATION CHART								
	Placement	1	2	3	4	5	6	7	8

MARKING CRITERIA: ★ = Still developing   ★★ = Progressing well   ★★★ = Excellent

Evaluation chart

PUPIL'S NAME	EVALUATION CHART				
	End of term 1	End of term 2	End of term 3	Final	Exam preparation

MARKING CRITERIA: ★ = Still developing   ★★ = Progressing well   ★★★ = Excellent